THE NEXT SETTLEMENT

Previous Winners of the Vassar Miller Prize in Poetry
Scott Cairns, Series Editor

Partial Eclipse by Tony Sanders
Selected by Richard Howard

Delirium by Barbara Hamby
Selected by Cynthia Macdonald

The Sublime by Jonathan Holden
Selected by Yusef Komunyakaa

American Crawl by Paul Allen
Selected by Sydney Lea

Soul Data by Mark Svenvold
Selected by Heather McHugh

Moving & St rage by Kathy Fagan
Selected by T. R. Hummer

A Protocol for Touch by Constance Merritt
Selected by Eleanor Wilner

The Perseids by Karen Holmberg
Selected by Sherod Santos

The Self as Constellation by Jeanine Hathaway
Selected by Madeline DeFrees

Bene-Dictions by Rush Rankin
Selected by Rosanna Warren

Losing and Finding by Karen Fiser
Selected by Lynne McMahon

The Black Beach by J. T. Barbarese
Selected by Andrew Hudgins

re-entry by Michael White
Selected by Paul Mariani

The Next Settlement

poems by
Michael Robins

2006 Winner, Vassar Miller Prize in Poetry

University of North Texas Press
Denton, Texas

©2007 Michael Robins

All rights reserved.
Printed in the United States of America.

10 9 8 7 6 5 4 3 2 1

Permissions:
University of North Texas Press
P.O. Box 311336
Denton, TX 76203-1336

The paper used in this book meets the minimum requirements of the
American National Standard for Permanence of Paper for Printed Library
Materials, z39.48.1984. Binding materials have been chosen for durability.

Library of Congress Cataloging-in-Publication Data

Robins, Michael, 1976–
   The next settlement : poems / by Michael Robins.
      p. cm. -- (Vassar Miller prize in poetry series ; no. 14)
   ISBN-13: 978-1-57441-225-3 (pbk. : alk. paper)
   ISBN-10: 1-57441-225-6 (pbk. : alk. paper)
   I. Title. II. Series.
   PS3618.O3178N49 2007
   811'.6--dc22

                           2006033999

The Next Settlement is Number 14 in the
Vassar Miller Prize in Poetry Series.

for DJM

Contents

ACKNOWLEDGMENTS

Grateful acknowledgment is made to the editors of the following journals where versions of these poems first appeared or are forthcoming:

Backwards City Review: "Exits"
Black Warrior Review: "Flanked by Postcards, Pieces of the Wall"
Boston Review: "Plunder"
Cimarron Review: "Maps of New Jersey Inside the Palm"
Court Green: "Last Days on Spaulding Street"
DIAGRAM: "Our Homes on the Same Street"
Gulf Coast: "Requiem for an Omitted Love Song (#70)"
Hubbub: "The Next Settlement"
LIT: "Still Life with Elephant," "Still Life with Gravestone," "Still Life with Steeple"
Make: "Notes Toward an Untitled Movie," "Welcome, Please Come In"
Meridian: "Kodachrome"
The National Poetry Review: "The Beautiful Corpse," "Introduction to Midsummer," "Lion's Tooth, Priest's Crown, Fairy Clock, Cankerwort, Swine's Snout, Pissenlit, Irish Daisy, Telltime, Monk's Head & Buttercup," "The Other Half of Red," "Queen of the Adriatic," "Small Hands at the Water's Edge," "This Item Traveled Miles to Reach You"
Octopus: "Ending with an Outward Glance," "Merely a Hearth in the Largest Room"
Pebble Lake Review: "The Cows Go Mulling Home," "Predilection"
Redactions: "Appraising Their Fine Threads," "Recurrent Dream" (I travel by horse . . .)
Rhino: "First Doubts in the Third Person"
Spinning Jenny: "Still Life with Steam Engine"
Third Coast: "The Merrymakers"
Unpleasant Event Schedule: "Recurrent Dream" (Of late, a riderless . . .), "Recurrent Dream" (Thumbs bounce before . . .), "Recurrent Dream" (Now that I stop . . .)
Verse: "Appearances," "We Are Small Under a Rumor of the Tongue"

Sincere thanks to my family, teachers, and friends.

I

Last Days on Spaulding Street

Reelection a rumor that we could believe,
I drank, I slept late despite a fear of looters.

When I was building a frame for our bed,
another arrived in the night & stole the stock

of a perfect lumber, prying away the nails.
Between praise & ruin, we began to tremble.

Candidacy, a promise that wouldn't keep,
my brother was due to return from the war.

Some had flags & some their yellow ribbons,
I divided so often among the open wine

that the memory closed, our blackened home.
I drank, I slept late, I dreamt a terrible lie.

Recurrent Dream

In a fanciful recess, paraded & pressed by hands,
they came to find a memento I thought slipped

behind the stand of cottonwoods, a dirge resung.
In a mirage whose architect is one, decoys glide

in a vestige stirred by light. My name is ruthless,
I claim I'm without pigment, fingerprints or marks.

The places to hide were few, fewer still the lives
unsnared in the brake of reeds, betrayal's lure.

Pastless, I feign my dance under deflected skies,
I reside in the company of considerable shovels.

Flanked by Postcards, Pieces of the Wall

Scholars dispute inscriptions on a limestone box,
the morning erupts again beside the river.
There's a history too in every backroom & cellar:
here is where they fast the pleasing flowers,
love me not. Here, where the crater is buried.
The whims of grown men leave boots everywhere,
the largest moon rock in Europe, splashed down
& paraded, could be mistaken for a small fist.
When the whitewash breaks, semaphores rise
from a faint glue beyond the horizon's grin.
They are flags, raised over parliament's shell,
they are arms, bound & dragged through a city.

Gray Gone Missing

& though a needle drops among the stacks
few are never found. Their absence stirs

a long speculation, their speculation breeds
the undying string of theories: someone

drinks from his umbrella along the beach,
the face beyond a crowded street, another

lives simply among the doorless pueblos.
These stories populate a mountain village

just beyond a cemetery rumored on the map.
How difficult to vanish in a daily event:

the cancer, accident, feet swept overboard.
A radio cracks somewhere in the morning,

the heavy rains yet another form of snow.
It takes a simple math when the depressed

go absent, though none wish the body found
where other cars are empty: casings, a floor

or vacant in a tree, snagged along the shore.
Their jackets are a sodden black that's hung

across the shoulders, the night as a thread
toward longevity, those things unspoken,

a secret knock, light behind a narrow slot
to bring the living closer to taking pleasure.

Poise

According to statisticians, a New Yorker's
snared a hundred times by the camera's eye.

My double is last to enter a room of guests
who crouch, mark time to surprise the one

I've met, learned to hate, to then forget.
Plotinus says symmetry is no prerequisite

for beauty, his own self-portrait cut in half.
When showing up at my door unannounced,

I've caught flashes among those strangers
as if I were a husband returned by the war.

Appraising Their Fine Threads

Return the glance, I understood
& should have answered better

than to trust again that spider
who trapped & left us for dead.

If our house is a web, then love
is the prey that pulls off escaped

(even rain is known to tear holes
in the garden of tended leaves).

Departure minus the intention,
our starts stiffen through remorse

& dreams find us newly wound
in a passage to leave the other full.

We ourselves spin a lovely silk,
never have we believed this well.

Plunder

The heart, which often seems a gangplank
teethed from its deck, lifts on the wavebreak

before sinking in the valley of dark waters.
How is it the eye squeezes slack or drinks

lavishly from the sea, an apparition below?
My kind is so full of shit our eyes grow dim,

brown their way through lies & then regret,
a dirt, a speck, a spark or spur, an ember.

For those washed to sea, the crabs feed first
on the eyes, then the loose flesh of a cheek

while the shark has its say in the undertow.
Should he circle low, the heart is already

a bleached stone, sockets, temporary home
for the small to mistake as a balanced shell.

Recurrent Dream

Thumbs bounce before the chin, the wrist
at rest inside the glove until the muscles tense

like the sleepers shaken by their sudden fall.
This fiction is the one I should never wake from,

adrift as if the legs were strangers, a kidney spun
twice, three times before sweetness fills the jaw.

A darkening unlike the others, one hand's bout
without a target, the perils gather around.

Inside the fist, the shell of a chestnut expands,
shivers & splits like a shroud from the body.

Appearances

For the hours in which a silhouette is cast,
the evening's kept awake by another form.

Now it's now again, the snow bears patterns
for the shapes who nearly meet in the snow.

Once a covered slope was manner for taking,
a profile for each rise in the conversation.

The streets under light are empty time again
for linen, tables & chairs of a festive spread.

Once I built a frame, hoarded convention
to counter the sound a hungry circle makes.

Evenings become figures, the lover sleeps
in a fold of white sheets & the appetite grows.

For the Piano Played at Sea

We sold each song for the pull
of present song, the bent hook

drawn through a muscled throat
& held, reverence of our breath.

The beauty in it all made waves,
receded. We sailed for the steam

of a maiden ship, white shirts
fluttered in our hands like flags.

We welcomed the polished deck,
the ripe note of its modern helm.

The Other Half of Red

If one had said her god was luck, her luck
was not all: *It was never meat nor drink . . .*

The one who runs all the way to the bank?
That was someone else, her ivory caught

in the manner of drafts, the train dismissed.
Lucy knocked for the boy to wake his dog,

out between cars, *Lucky, not long now . . .*
Steam rose into the night, the white cinder

of the blessed ruined a dozen cotton shirts
before leaving threadbare coats as scenery.

Though she was revived, though she too
passed the valley teeming with hay, Lucy

feared not the nested sun above the incubator.
Her luck was shepherd, she shouldn't want

a service honed, first among tuckered pews
for she lacks the sound machine for sleep.

Lucy was tardy in knocking for the boy,
her terminal empty, wasn't torn from her seat

when the others were scattered like petals
through a cornfield. *Might this, too, be fortune?*

She, the adult, put half her coffers on red,
a promising outcome of the lot. For her luck

so loved the world, Lucy repelled hours
that they might slow the birds that flutter

between the tenuous chambers of her heart.
A short sentence in the Bible, none could make

tears enough to render her cries convincing:
luck would overflow the days of her life.

Recurrent Dream

You sway from the lip of your bed, an edge
to a drawer to the suitcase left at the door

& so forth. Inside the box is a smaller box.
The morning begins blue, handles, departs

in flutters, the entire city block now level.
From a chain on your neck is a plastic heart,

within the heart is a shape unlike the heart.
Despite your clasp, a common resolution,

this dream commences with a flash, gasp,
an echo before impact in the elevator's shaft.

Maps of New Jersey Inside the Palm

In my dream life I only read, never write
nor make exact change before a bus arrives.
Daily librarians fear the sprinkler system;
the crossing guard, too late, notices the boy.
Sometimes my chance life's a small prison
to incarcerate the faces of school annuals.
One would think the day as slow progress
but even the reverie thickens behind the eye.
Temperatures rise in the candle factories,
my dream life grows comprehensive, lists,
allergies to afflict my neighbors & friends.
Another day, another remnant from a town
whose name at night we sound using cups,
spoons, our plans to the bars of a window.

The Cows Go Mulling Home

I fed in your pasture, the others
were soured company to the sky.

I assumed the error of mouths,
your pastoral broad as the moon

while the cats fray a low grass,
birds taking up the form of wings.

Having one long key for the gate,
I might resist the heated fence

where expectation sets on the lip,
catches within the nest of the throat.

I considered proof of my flight,
that you'd be quite pleased to see.

Predilection

The border's on the brink, the reports
disposed with each speculation of what.

Last night, nearly obscure, we heard
another bed through the ceiling creak

as if our enemy extends a narrow mirror
to remind us mediation's not unique.

Now the stirrings advance at half-mast,
a bridge that binds two shores together.

I listened this morning to a buzz embed
in the purse of a spider who wasn't home.

All those hostages are believed freed
or dead, their blindfolds lifted in the air.

Exits

We've heard it said the earth rotates into light,
that oceans are tied between here & the moon.
We stay indoors, where each drawer is a bed
for postcards & portraits, the wall a calendar
where Tuesdays are noted like mounds of ash.
The revolving door is neither good nor bad,
we mark unforeseen leisure, the sneaker wave
amid waves, gusts in a wind among buildings.
The sun is a canvas for the famous painters,
our shelves, empty, a minor residence for dust.
Later, the neighbor will say how good we were.

Matters of the Art

I dread the little death, stand back
across the hillside memorial of a city.

A swirl of birds, beneath the churl
a music drums, its singer a suicide

in the park or is the tune redundant,
a shot flashing barnside on a lark?

I clean the closet of papers & lead,
tightly pressed in matching luggage.

The promise of travel is a promise
found in the red, wet circle of a shirt.

II

In Some Midwestern Country

where the living gather up the food,
ignite the posts & beset our house,
pleasure dies in every emptied room.
Glow, we ease debris from the curb,
the engines lead us toward reunion
overhead, celestial, a drifting station
to cross the bright spark of a planet.
Our souvenirs are sold as if spoken,
auctioneers in the bed of their trucks.
The scales zero, we spiral the stair
built by a will of our master's hands:
overbid, obsessive, miscalculating
how long the news of our departure
takes to reach the farthest visible star.

Still Life with Steeple

An adhesive, no less important than buttons. Buttons make the world go round, an incisor at bay like the plastic fork, the mattress nailed to the springs & vice versa. The First Congregation is a gray stone in the footing, shadow of an early bird, the year 1867. The first apple carved by worms. I lift their bodies from the avenue, eight years old, walking to a bus stop in the rain. There are no buses in the year 1867, or plastic forks. I am the squirrel afraid of heights, I know. I am the pious who tremble during prayer.

Lion's Tooth, Priest's Crown, Fairy Clock, Cankerwort, Swine's Snout, Pissenlit, Irish Daisy, Telltime, Monk's Head & Buttercup

The gesture is startling, a sudden column
of light that punctuates the month, the flowers
spread in our kitchen. There isn't a bottle
of wine in the house nor have I found the time
to respond. The purplish stalks, uprooted,
revel in the water of their wire-handled jars,
coup d'état between a common week & pollen,
a singe of amber lips. There're countless ways
toward the implied you: a wand, a magic hare
or when we raise both & keep them there.
Take your weed, these pomegranates instead,
a story embedded where the needle weaves
inside the spiraled groove: *See the names turn?*
Because I enjoy a simple distraction, because
confession suits me better, I overlook the game,
the ball & shells, a color crushed in her hand
& unveiled. The noon hour fits inside a sleeve,
there isn't a pinot gris in the house or a soldier
out of uniform. I don't have a pomegranate
but they sound delicious like a petaled robe,
nectar by the minute. In our breakfast nook
I'm showing symptoms of a symptom, a fume
that grows across a floorboard of the room,
a careless spark, a split second, an ardent ruin.

Still Life with Gravestone

You have to return the book, whether you've read it or not, though every face, even the dead & dying, seems more likely to take another inch from the sheet that curtains the room. People die every day: a radio poised over the tub, the piano that spins by a rope, disputes that find a cold resolve. Think *banana peel.* The skin loosens its grip, the veins map a branch across the instep. You can't mend the binding. You can't pay the fines or feed the thinning air. The meter will soon expire, so move along, move along.

Recurrent Dream

I travel by horse, weighed by swollen forks
that shift & startle the prowl of hungry dogs.

From the unlit side of the ordinary street,
they emerge on course to an elegant party.

I believe I recognize their attire, wonder why
invitations fall short of the answering machine.

I remember none of these buildings, the city
in which the tree is adorned with cans & string

so we might reach a voice of the never home.
I record my questions instead of breathing.

A Feather in One's Cap

A cardinal slices through the afternoon,
the wet beads against a cluttered bed

resound a downfall. Those days I'd floss
I'd also smoke, my calling served to coax

embodied choirs from spectrums of red.
Triumph is the business of roaming ants:

they'll clean animals who cross their path.
Expressions tire, rain displaces fellaheen

from our yard. Between green mileposts
the lost glove thins like the good news

our savior drives home beneath his whip.
A quarter century without the umbrella

I never thought I'd purchase, imagine
how I'd have to wrestle the air to keep it.

This Item Traveled Miles to Reach You

The wooden bridge is where we left it,
errant planks knotting the water's debris.
Decided on a walk, we divide on the air
caught more with seed than the breeze
allows. All morning the light flew, houses
empty albeit our two exhausted bodies.
Again, our conversation difficult at best
where we stay the split shade of two trees,
the strum of a different summer month
where the theory of streams is full & holds
a static course. We say the waters rise
or fall & it's a fine thing to revise our lives.
I welcome the truth as four-letter words,
say *injured source* to say it the twelfth
& thirteenth times. I fold a fragile boat,
replay that vessel floating from our range.

Still Life with Envelope

The letters keep arriving, misgiving & pleas, though I'd rather be the landlocked shore in lieu of the East, an Atlantic seaboard. The gulls beat sand, inland fountains & the Opera House, the spires that take turns to strike the numbered counts of the hour. If you lived there you'd be loam by now, rubbed raw, unstamped from the contraption that gives & takes an ardent hope. You record each wish in writing from abroad, you'll take peace of mind & hunt the torso, an empty floor, my name from the door.

Introduction to Midsummer

Less suited for sewing, the rotor
coughs to mow imperfect lines,

half circles turned upon the edge
where treehomes collapse in wood.

First times are the modern rage,
so it goes looking over shoulders.

The keen nose follows the creek
along the rotting fence, rooftops

cowered under a faithful change
of seasons, a back-to-back failing.

Such discretion between flowers,
the stems that realign another color.

Recurrent Dream

Now that I stop completing the final bank
before landings mislay in flame, I'm addicted

to glaciers & the riptide, a body's length ahead
as the blue relics roll the crescent of the eyes.

There's forgery far dire than obsession with I:
the foot should you whirl toward the bellow,

stifled & towed low in the ice-covered depths.
Savior hindered by breath, spectator with no raft,

I rehearse a replica of repeated deaths, the oar,
the mere stroke versus a fear of pulling down.

Requiem for an Omitted Love Song (#70)

If I wake an hour late the orbit of the day
begins to wobble, entire, a body begun small
& softening the higher it falls. On the surface
the sun is hot, but here no more than warm
& I'll stay inside, away from light & ice cream.
I insist that you keep me posted on the news
in the East. If I dig just enough I can touch
a foundation with my spade, I can hear a radio
repeat *cache* & *destruction* at the top of the hour
before the ultimatum is aired or the refrain
that delivers time & place from a narrative
long ago: we held hands until they bedsored,
too much love & no place to sling our hats.
The nights were starry, but memory tumbles
in the swirled thought of day. This is one
mistake but the mistake repeats out-of-print.
If one can feel a color, mine is a hint of rouge
when the neighborhood cat neglects a visit
& leaves me alone with the evening's paper:
I don't know why she stands before the dozer
or why she slipped. No matter the cups of tea
my voice won't sway into the lowest range
of a Stephin Merritt phrase. Excuse me please
if my signature drifts, the letters are verbatim:
the moon rises, a stomach thins in the night
& only the epitaph changes. Though I might
assume this evening's dream, forgive me
if I don't use your name. I miss you. You look
lovely, spread in the sky & rushing toward me.

Still Life with Steam Engine

The first is recorded in Wales, the first turn of the century, the heart of a horse replaced by water, to bring the workers home. I invented the passenger train without passengers. It shuffled toward the washed-out track. The details exist because I've seen a photograph, I've had many dreams: the skull of a horse in the Syrian, the angled break in a bridge, the dangling in between. I invent a survivor, the nearly widowed in the shape of a cloud, the flat chance on a scalded tongue. There the hounds smell the shore, a diver searches the seamless water for a misshapen valve. Now I'm tracing the depth & density of skid marks: the broken tree, the blame, my few hobbies, a guardrail gone astray.

We Are Small Under a Rumor of the Tongue

We were awoken by the flood, drops of night
inside the larvae when something's overturned
our log. Blind are collective relics, inch to inch
where those have gone for sugar in a kitchen.
We have so many legs. They begin at the knee,
extend across the air as if for an empty glass
in the darkness of a room. The workers gnaw
within the circles between our jaws, their world
a narrow stair cut tall & back without a railing.
Larvae or pupae what's the difference? They're
ours, white at birth, they'll fight until they die.
A wind thwarts the grass, footpaths that tumble
like the branch end to end toward other yards,
other towns. Underground, we pile mounds
to protect our queen, our mother sealed inside
her chamber. We carry twenty times our weight.

Recurrent Dream

Of late, a riderless cycle quits the nearby row,
drifts from my father's call into a battle cry.

Now & again I'll insinuate the dying pulse
in the shape of a casual acquaintance or one

who spoke an hour in advance of my arrival,
smoke forthcoming from his skin-stripped flank.

Spotlights skirt the underbelly of the clouds,
at times a threadbare voice drapes repeated lies.

The row allays to the field of hay & arrows
where a dozen possibilities whistle past target.

Still Life with Elephant

Unlike the bear, who walks the unpolished figure of an eight, my neurosis is the sharp corners, a right angle at the door into a liquor store. My knees drop anchor under clear skies, the ankle cracks, my Achilles' waits in the oval rope for a hungry dog, the fingerprint in a swollen pupil. Here is my empty bucket. Here, a trunk bent to listen. Notice the stretch marks on my hips, how an artist can embody the common frailty. Let them say, *He was his worst critic, his own sidekick. He watched his life from a peanut gallery.* Let them say, *In the end he remembered very little, a distant corner, his one, tropical shirt that hung in the closet.*

Kodachrome

What you think were sheep are white bags,
spilled from their knots the rake's debris.

Owners throw their sticks, not for the dog
but for the piked seeds in the chestnut tops.

Move on, memory, image inside a silver box,
an ambling pair in silhouette, the horse's maw.

The wires appraise breadth, a trampoline too
should a blue note settle like nervous wings.

How you batter your lashes for the single tree
that towers the valley of a river, fields & wine.

Small Hands at the Water's Edge

We couldn't remember if we'd touched a goat
or if we wondered if we ever would. Indeed

we studied to resist confession among strangers,
or did we only mention the dead of the sea,

how some were still buckled to their seats?
Beginning with mother, our devoted friends

were lovely, the women with whom we lived.
Was it they who wept while the deer sped

farther into the forest? Like suspicion & sin
we resumed a life among the bungalows

where animals stopped to rest in the darkness.
It was they who pinched our pollen trove. There,

against the shore from where they'd come,
we kindled the fires for whom we didn't know.

Recurrent Dream

Every action is met with a misknown reaction:
the smiles refuse to shatter, jokes unroll in Latin.

Our friends are friends but different in the eyes.
Dice tumble down & it's hard getting out of jail,

the length of each yarn strung to a pair of needles
& at their end a scarf, maybe the heart of a doll.

You are not you, he is not me, no one knows
what the others are drinking, whether it's instinct

that compels a bird to shrill over nestlings spilled.
In accordance with rules, something must lose.

The Merrymakers

We have had, possessed, another to caress
& this unveiling persists to send us early

into sleep that is not sleep but empty vessels,
the breath a feast with no apparent measure.

Who needs an exacting diet when there's history
to snack on? Who, in the body, needs loyalties

professed in arms secured around that other?
It would be easier if we did not exist, to say

we never heard the peal of the chapel bell.
We do, in the night without our vow, or rest.

Notes Toward an Untitled Movie

A summer better known for storm chasers,
some recalled home as the shape of corn.

None of our horses survived. We knew this
before the final, finished tally of our own.

Hungry again, the scavenger in us done,
our afterlife began with memory, the rib,

with hope from bed to the red bark of a tree
whose trunk bends below a swollen river.

Some survivors claimed that sky as god,
angry, pushing steeples through their roofs,

water through a levee, the house downstream
towards the span of the last standing bridge.

Until then we could only remember this:
we'd been to southern Illinois exactly twice.

We compared our skin to clouds, to the air,
bewildered at first by an unveiled hip. Open,

out, the umbrellas were wings uninformed,
we covered our shame with sturdy boards.

Our time ended not with pearls. Spirals
continue to batter this day neither inland

nor out to sea. We were sorry about that.
We had never been so sorry about anything.

Our Homes on the Same Street

The shy distance between two points
is distance yet, envious, blue veins

where a needle takes the inner arm
to the pumping traction of the heart.

Hair grown around the watering hole,
I take turns with lemons, the scissor.

Our picnics consist of ultimatums:
I support the cause, I'm unimproved,

the legs of insects are spoils closed
in the splayed battlefield of the palm.

There's adequate water for the journey,
stainless thimbles to fill at the pump.

Recurrent Dream

I'm an antique chassis wheeling forwards,
lamps amiss, time imposed on the pail of brick

while towns dissolve entire, lower to their knees
& crawl to a village that is a regiment of tents.

Some claim we dream in fields relieved from color,
so why these footfalls to a flaxen box, dimecards

bearing memento to a doorway's copper hinge?
The stars of generals canter from a historic battle,

cannons dampen, the springs of a snare uncurl
as a light flags to sheen, a yellow preceding green.

Queen of the Adriatic

Snow falls like ash on the crest of the bridge.
It's night, we've yet to eat through the vine

of a glass shaped like seedless fruit. We agree
that women are a history behind good men,

that good men live inside every prison gate.
Uneven, the chapel's pale mosaic crawls

into the sea. *Accumulate*, we say, the days
raked from a bench drawn as chair, as bed,

the teetered stair below a crude oval of rope.
For those things adorned my eyes are magnets:

chiffon & bells, a wine flush against the lips
or the prosaic waves, blind from San Michele.

No heaven there, no mirth. Of all the promises
circling Venice, I'm the one bent at my knee

to clear a modern composer's grave, the notes
harnessed to the earth by garlands & snow.

We're hungry, the flowers are gray, we beckon
a reprieve from winter. This street is a spiral

leading nowhere. *No*, I've lied: I'm so happy
that I take photos to later hold the broken bird.

Redundant Acts as Acts of Progress

Gathered fireside despite the spark,
the crack, the gleam that transferred

a buoyant shadow among the trees.
Change, an inevitable pacing of days,

the pair of lungs inflating, deflated.
My perfect moments are in retrospect,

happiness a room filled with string,
snare, a wind to lift some music there.

All those days I'd go over with pen
what was traced already with lead.

The tree blushed an innermost ring,
I made nothing to show I was feeling.

The Presence of a Sudden Tone

I bore sunflowers at the funeral, trophy wreaths
to the door of my first date, lace of toenail red.

There were seasons driven for sheer seeming
of a posture routing east. The skyline changed

& I invested stock to divide the proper things:
my right, my left that fairer sex my surest love,

sobriety, a day pent well & a day well spent.
Reasons lapse, plums split & sink in the grass.

The bells recede above a corner, façades & lanes
we won't revisit in stride, the church's glass

singular for opalescence, no sizable greatness,
details small enough to mound, to trek through.

First Doubts in the Third Person

He brushed aside the question, an actress
to her husband the actor, *What's this perfume?*

His wife will leave him for another movie,
three friends she'll enjoy instead of him.

Some claim our worlds transpire in threes:
Should it begin you're lucky should it end . . . .

He reads three letters addressed to his wife,
feels the burden of glue, each envelope shut.

This is married life, he says to the dark aisle
on the way from one chair to another chair.

Often he dreams he's alone inside a theater
that is really a photo on a third couple's wall.

Awake, he turns over his wife's perfect hair
to see, just in case, if something is written.

He remembers this happens before it happens.

Recurrent Dream

The weather's cold to bathe, a present gray
over mouths I neglect to nourish, summoned

by nostalgia for the aperture of a highway:
I tell her one, dark secret that isn't even mine.

Across the roof, a stethoscope presses sound,
at the door a remnant & its twin rap the pulse.

The clouds shift down in slivers along the road
trailing to & fro below the house, dying out

during sleep, the way I claim I'd like to go
when I'd rather stay, or talk, or feed the past.

Ending with an Outward Glance

Today, late summer, the long hour's spent
in the company of letters, ribbons & mulch,

a simple, wooden cross for the recent dead.
Once a year, I smoked the day at the grave

of one who vanished beneath his cancer.
Now I'm less bold, how much the wiser

for thoughts of a world washing its hands.
Twice I knew a photograph to be the last,

when things that needed saying were said.
Across the road, the stones are a clean slate.

My grandmother, who has no grave, spoke
as if her photos were taken only yesterday.

On the Hour Beneath the Music

Every town should house a museum of torture,
the obvious guillotine, a pyramid to straddle
with rope, weights to tie & drape the ankles.
The horse, which drags the body through streets,
is a mirror whose timely distance resembles less
a broken body, less the punishment for crime
than the carousel that turns with the century.
The façade adorned as a carpet ride, dwarves
& maiden tales, smoke over a gingerbread home.
In every town the pigeons startle, turn, resettle
atop a pedestal of the saint known for kindness.
Once, men were caged & hung above the square.

Swinging Doors

She put herself in a nursing home,
her mind a corridor of closing belief.

The days in which she habitually cast?
Out of season, swerving out of town.

In one frame they're turquoise heels,
her collar swung low & for the asking.

She turned freshly painted cigarettes,
lipstick red & full of a brilliant element.

She was able to populate the present
in memory, she stole fires from a god.

The Next Settlement

Grief repairs grief, there's bounty
for the hunter whose careless aim

mirrors a second hairlined sight,
set & cocked, reigned by the finger.

The happy trigger points three back,
its blame persists as does the river.

At the banks a fishing line slips,
sinks, reels in the focused attention

joined in the arm by solid shoulders,
the deserving kind to better times.

Merely a Hearth in the Largest Room

Their eyes like those of some joyless animal,
the kings & queens suggest a farce in portraits,
cloth in lieu of garlands if standing chaste.
Gunpowder changed the sword, epaulettes
the decorative things inside a translucent box.
For each modest cluster of chimney & frame
the spires rise above the town, beneath one
they found a cellar full of skull & femur stacked.
Nothing grows just under the eyes, hollow,
the castle gutted by fire, rebuilt & gutted twice.
Before yesterday, I'd never seen a family tree
that wasn't a root spreading wide to the living.

The Beautiful Corpse

Initially there were geese that refused
their passage south, some intents that rose

in the city's plume. During the first hours
I sifted through America, her bare gifts,

a chronology of me, then you. Time passed
& then your dog was born, her eyes closed,

bestowed upon in milk while the runt
of the litter stole toward the fallow fields.

It's a beautiful corpse that no one can see
inside me, in my wallet a photo to prove

I was wrapped in towels the size of birds.
Hopelessly hopeful, I'm trying to remember

how I lost my tail, if when we met the cloth
revealed a surgeon's even thread. I offered

my theory of roadsides, that the dead, taken
in the flash, climb incessantly the stairs

where a blue sky above neither widens
nor gains in density. I was sorry even then

for my need to apologize, wished a capacity
no worse than a place where fire is. That men

would die surprised very few, but many
returned in the fold of our country's flag.